THE ELEMENTS

Cadmium

Allan Cobb

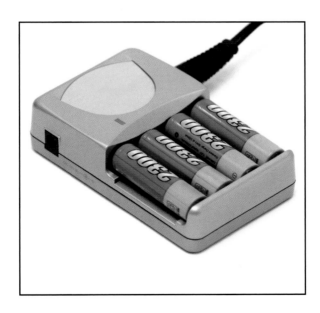

mc **Marshall Cavendish**
Benchmark

New York

Marshall Cavendish Benchmark
99 White Plains Road
Tarrytown, New York 10591

www.marshallcavendish.us

Library of Congress Cataloging-in-Publication Data

Cobb, Allan B.
Cadmium / Allan Cobb.
p. cm. -- (The Elements)
Includes index.
ISBN 978-0-7614-2686-8
1. Cadmium--Juvenile literature. I. Title.

QD181.C3C63 2007
546'.662--dc22

2006051790

1 6 5 4 3 2

Printed in Malaysia

Picture credits
Front cover: Shutterstock
Back cover: Shutterstock

Corbis: Lester V. Bergman 17, Erik De Castro/Reuters 13, Kevin Flemming 27,
Richard T. Nowitz 14t, Charles E. Rotkin 23
National Library of Medicine: 12
Shutterstock: Amber Bradley 18, Vladimir Breytberg 9, Sascha Burkard 25bl, Stephen Coburn 7,
Kameel 4 U 24, Melissa King 8, Anne Kitzman 25r, Adrian Matthiassen 21, Roman Milert 5, Ronen 1, 6
Science Photo Library: Andrew Lambert Photography 30, Ken Cavanagh 26, Department of Physics, Imperial College 10,
Ben Johnson 11, Max Planck Institute for Metallurgy 3, 15, Vaughan Melzer/JVZ 22, Sam Ogden 19, Rich Treptow 4
Teck Cominco Limited: 14b

Series created by The Brown Reference Group plc.
Designed by Sarah Williams
www.brownreference.com

Contents

What is cadmium?

Cadmium is a relatively rare metal but it is used for many different purposes. Cadmium in its pure form is silvery white with a bluish color. The metal is very soft and can be easily cut with a steel knife. Cadmium is also a very malleable metal. A malleable substance can easily be pounded flat to form thin, flexible sheets.

The nature of cadmium

An element is a simple substance that cannot be divided into other substances. There are 90 elements that occur naturally in Earth's crust. Compared to the other elements, cadmium is rare— 66 other elements are more common.

Pure cadmium does not exist in nature. Instead the metal is combined with other elements as compounds. A compound is a substance formed when two or more elements combine during a chemical reaction. Cadmium metal is purified only by humans. It does not have any odor or taste and it is very poisonous.

Inside atoms

Everything in the universe consists of tiny particles called atoms. Atoms are the building blocks of all the elements. They are very small—far too small to be seen with a microscope. The period at the end of this sentence would cover about 250 billion atoms.

Atoms are made up of three even smaller particles: electrons, protons, and neutrons. Electrons have a negative charge and protons have a positive charge.

Pure cadmium is a bluish metal. It is too soft and poisonous to use in its pure form. Instead small amounts are added to other metals.

Neutrons do not have a charge at all—they are neutral. The protons and neutrons are located at the center of the atom. They form a core called the nucleus. The electrons are much smaller and lighter than the other particles. Electrons move around the nucleus. They are positioned in layers, or shells, that surround the nucleus.

An atom always has the same number of protons and electrons inside. As a result, an atom is neutral. That is because the positive charges of the protons are canceled out by the negative charges of the electrons.

Cadmium compounds are used in solar panels. These devices convert sunlight into electricity. Making electricity in this way does not produce pollution.

The cadmium atom

Different elements have a different number of protons and electrons in their atoms. The number of protons in the nucleus of an atom is its atomic number. The atoms of one element have a unique atomic number. The atomic number of a cadmium atom is 48, so there are 48 protons in the nucleus. No other element has this number of protons in its atoms.

In a piece of pure cadmium, the atoms all have an equal number of protons and electrons. So each cadmium atom has 48 electrons moving around the nucleus.

Atomic mass number

There is another number used to describe the structure of an atom. The atomic mass number is the total number of particles in the atom's nucleus—both protons and neutrons.

Cadmium atoms have a range of atomic mass numbers. They all have 48 protons in their nucleus, but the number of neutrons varies from atom to atom.

One of the main uses of cadmium is in rechargeable batteries. When the batteries are dead, they can be recharged by running an electric current through them. As a result, they can be used again and again.

CADMIUM ATOM

Nucleus

First shell
Second shell
Third shell
Fourth shell
Fifth shell

The number of protons in the nucleus of an atom is the same as the number of electrons moving around the nucleus. Every cadmium atom has 48 protons in the nucleus and 48 electrons positioned around it. The electrons are located in 5 layers called electron shells. There are 2 electrons in the inner shell, 8 electrons in the second shell, 18 electrons in the third shell, 18 electrons in the fourth shell, and 2 in the outer shell.

An electric car powered by a large battery that contains cadmium.

A cadmium atom with 62 neutrons in its nucleus has an atomic mass number of 110 (48 + 62 = 110). An atom with 68 neutrons has an atomic mass number of 114. Versions of atoms with different atomic mass numbers are called isotopes. The average atomic mass number for all cadmium atoms is 112.

A reactive element

Cadmium is fairly reactive so it forms compounds with other elements easily. Cadmium reacts mainly with nonmetal elements. Common nonmetals are oxygen, carbon, and chlorine. There are many differences between metals and nonmetals. The main difference is that metals, including cadmium, have just a few electrons in their outer shell. An atom's outer shell can hold eight electrons. Most nonmetals have outer shells that are nearly full.

During reactions, atoms lose, gain, or share electrons so that their outer shells become full. Cadmium reacts with nonmetals to form compounds called salts. Salts form when electrons move from metal atoms to nonmetal atoms during a reaction. The most common cadmium salt is cadmium sulfide (CdS). That compound is formed when cadmium atoms (Cd) and sulfur atoms (S) react with each other.

Special characteristics

In many ways, cadmium is similar to zinc, the metal that is positioned above cadmium in the periodic table. For example, both metals are soft and easy to bend. Cadmium also reacts with other elements in similar ways as zinc. The two metals are often found in the same ores. An ore is a natural compound that contains a useful amount of an element or another substance.

The reason for the similarity between cadmium and zinc is because the electrons inside their atoms are arranged in the same ways. However, there are differences. Cadmium is more reactive than zinc, and it forms more complex molecules. A molecule is a combination of atoms

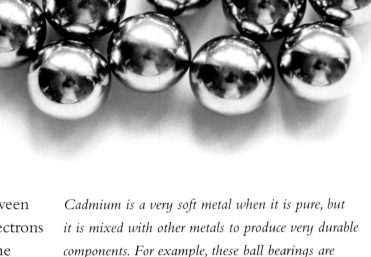

Cadmium is a very soft metal when it is pure, but it is mixed with other metals to produce very durable components. For example, these ball bearings are coated with cadmium so they roll around without being damaged or bent out of shape.

that are bonded together. The bonds that hold molecules together are formed during chemical reactions.

Transition metals

Cadmium is one of 38 elements that are called transition metals. Like other metals, transition metals are malleable, ductile (can be pulled into wires), and are good at carrying heat and electricity. However, transition metals are different from all other elements because of the

CADMIUM FACTS	
● Chemical symbol	Cd
● Atomic number	48
● Atomic mass number	112
● Melting point	610 °F (321 °C)
● Boiling point	1409 °F (765 °C)
● Density:	8.69 grams per cubic cm (8.69 times the density of water)

way they react. Other elements react using just the electrons in the outer shells of their atoms. Transition metals do this too, but they also react using electrons located in the second-to-last shell. This ability allows cadmium and other transition metals to react in more ways with the atoms of some other elements.

Melting point

Cadmium has a fairly low melting point compared to other metals. A mixture of metals is called an alloy, and cadmium is often mixed with other metals. Cadmium alloys often have a lower melting point than a similar alloy without cadmium

in it. An example is solder, which is melted onto metal objects and bonds them together as it cools into a solid. Cadmium is used in solder to lower the melting point.

Isotopes of cadmium

Cadmium has eight isotopes. Isotopes are atoms that have the same number of protons and electrons but have a different number of neutrons. Because neutrons have a neutral charge, the number of

A blowtorch is used to join metal pipes. The heat from the flame melts an alloy called solder. The solder fills the gaps around the join between the pipes. Solder is an alloy of lead, tin, and cadmium.

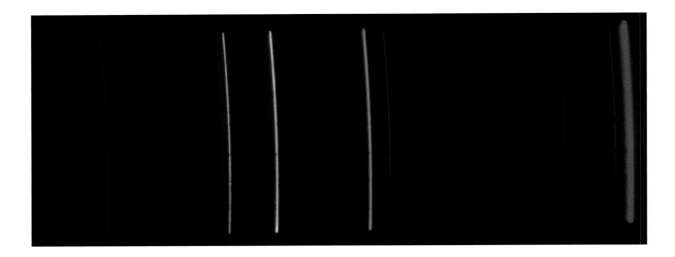

neutrons does not affect the overall charge of the atom. But it does affect the atomic mass number.

The two most common isotopes of cadmium have atomic mass numbers of 112 and 114. These are called cadmium-112 (Cd-112) and cadmium-114 (Cd-114). These two isotopes make up half of all cadmium atoms. There are three other stable isotopes of cadmium: Cd-108, Cd-110, and Cd-111. These forms are less common. Together they make up about a quarter of all cadmium atoms.

Radioactive cadmium

A stable isotope is one with a nucleus that does not break apart easily. Three cadmium isotopes are unstable. Cd-106, Cd-113, and Cd-116 make up a little under a quarter of all cadmium atoms. The nuclei in their atoms break apart, or decay. The decay produces radiation and heat. Unstable isotopes are said to be

Colored light is produced by a cadmium atom when it is heated. This exact range of colors, or spectrum, is only produced by cadmium atoms.

radioactive. Cadmium's unstable isotopes decay very slowly and release only small amounts of radiation.

DID YOU KNOW?

A cadmium atom emits light when it is heated. The colors in this light are unique to cadmium. Light is made up of waves. The light's color is defined by the wavelength, or the distance from the top of one wave to the top of the next. In 1927, the International Conference of Weights and Measures decided to define the exact length of a meter (39 inches) using the light produced by cadmium. Red light from cadmium atoms was selected as the definition of a meter (1 m = 1,553,164.13 wavelengths). Today, however, the meter is defined differently. It is the distance light travels in just under 300 millionths of a second.

Cadmium in nature

Cadmium is very rare in nature and only occurs in small quantities. Most cadmium is found in the mineral greenockite, which is made up of cadmium sulfide (CdS). Greenockite is almost always found mixed in with the mineral sphalerite, which is composed of zinc sulfide (ZnS).

Cadmium compounds

Cadmium is never found in its pure form in nature. It always occurs bonded to other elements. The two most common cadmium compounds are cadmium sulfate and cadmium chloride. However, these two compounds are almost never found in rocks. That is because they both dissolve in water easily, and water trickling through rocks washes the compounds away. The cadmium compounds end up in the ocean as a tiny part of the salts dissolved in seawater. Cadmium sulfide does not dissolve, so that is the most common cadmium compound that occurs as a solid in rocks.

Cadmium forms some other very complex compounds and is found in a variety of minerals. Because cadmium is so rare, many of these unusual minerals are also very rare.

Cadmium sources

Most pure cadmium is extracted from ores that also contain zinc. Cadmium is also found in lead, mercury, and copper ores.

Cadmium can be found as impurities in phosphate minerals. (These compounds contain phosphorus and oxygen.) Some phosphate minerals are used to make plant fertilizers. If any of these minerals contain even just a tiny amount of cadmium, they will make the plants poisonous.

Sphalerite, a mineral containing mainly zinc sulfide, is a source of cadmium compounds. When zinc is extracted from the mineral, small amounts of cadmium are separated at the same time.

The discovery of cadmium

Cadmium is very difficult to find. It is estimated that 1,000 tons (900 tonnes) of rock contains only 7 ounces (200 g) of cadmium. It would take five tons of rock to have enough cadmium to make a thumbtack.

Rare but still there

Because it is so rare, cadmium was unknown until the nineteenth century. The metal was discovered by the German scientist Friedrich Stromeyer (1776–1835) in 1817. Stromeyer was researching zinc. He found cadmium as an impurity in zinc carbonate. Zinc carbonate, known as calamine, was a common medicine during Stromeyer's time. It is still used in some lotions today. Stromeyer found impure zinc carbonate would change color when heated but pure zinc carbonate would not. He extracted the impurity, which he

Friedrich Stromeyer discovered cadmium. He also studied the compounds used in early medicines.

found to be a metal similar to zinc. He named the new metal cadmium from *cadmia*, which is the Latin for "calamine."

Fellow discoverers

Two other German scientists, K.S.L. Hermann and J.C.H. Roloff, also discovered cadmium about the same time as Stromeyer. They were examining the gases produced when zinc oxide was heated. They discovered a new element in the gases that was most likely cadmium.

DID YOU KNOW?

Although cadmium compounds were first discovered in the medicine calamine, it is very poisonous. However, cadmium iodide was used as a medicine until about 100 years ago. It treated rashes and swollen joints and glands.

Producing cadmium

A miner holds ore dug from a mine on an island in the Philippines. The ore contains copper, zinc, and a tiny amount of cadmium.

Because cadmium is found in nature in very small quantities, it is difficult to mine and produce pure cadmium. Cadmium compounds are often found mixed in with the ores of other metals. As a result, pure cadmium is usually purified when other metals are purified.

Cadmium in ores

Most of the cadmium produced is a byproduct of processing the mineral sphalerite (zinc sulfide). A byproduct is something that is made during the production of something else. Sphalerite is processed, and the zinc is extracted. Since cadmium is also present in the mineral it is also extracted during refining. In most sphalerite ores, there is about 400 times as much zinc as cadmium.

Most zinc and cadmium is extracted from the ore by a process called electrolysis. The ore is crushed and dropped into a strong liquid acid. The acid reacts with the metal compounds, which dissolve in the acid. Then huge electric currents are

Cadmium and many other metals can be recovered and reused from batteries at a recycling center.

passed through the acid. The electricity splits the cadmium and zinc atoms from their compounds, making pure metals.

The top producers of cadmium in the world are China, Japan, and Korea. Other countries that produce large quantities of cadmium include Canada, Mexico, the United States, India, and Peru.

From recycled metals

Large quantities of pure cadmium are recovered from garbage. Nickel-cadmium batteries contain a lot of cadmium. Recycling these batteries keeps waste cadmium out of the environment. Cadmium pollution can cause harm to living things, including humans.

Another source of recycled cadmium is the steel industry. Some steel is coated in cadmium to stop it from rusting. The dust from processing steel contains a lot of cadmium, which can be reused.

Red Dog mine on the northern coast of Alaska produces zinc and cadmium.

Chemistry and compounds

In the periodic table, cadmium is located below zinc and above mercury. All three of these metals have similar chemical properties. This similarity is a result of the way electrons are arranged inside the atoms of the elements. All three elements have two electrons in their outer electron shells. The outer shells have room for six more electrons. However, all the other shells in these atoms are full of electrons.

Zinc, mercury, and cadmium all lose two electrons during chemical reactions. During a reaction, the two outer electrons leave the atom and move to the atom of another element. As a result, the three metals form similar compounds.

Ionic compounds

Cadmium reacts and forms compounds by giving its two outer electrons to one or two other atoms. When an atom loses or gains an electron it becomes an ion. Ions have a charge because they have a different number of electrons than protons. An atom that loses an electron becomes

Tiny particles of cadmium dust are photographed using a powerful microscope. Pure cadmium like this does not stay pure for long. It quickly reacts with oxygen and compounds in the air.

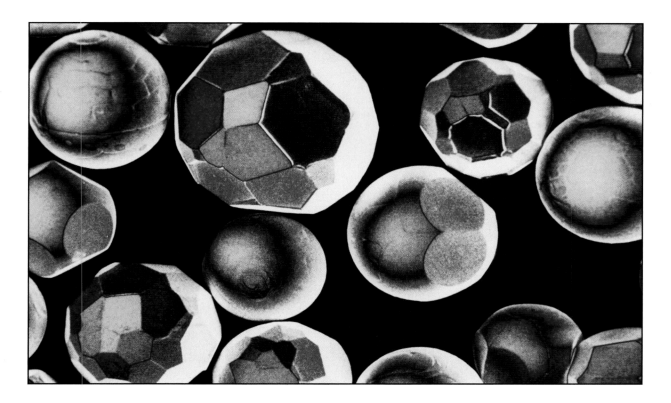

ATOMS AT WORK

Cadmium is more reactive than zinc because atoms of cadmium are larger than zinc atoms. An atom's negatively-charged electrons are held in place by the positively-charged protons in the nucleus. In cadmium atoms, the outer electrons, which take part in chemical reactions are further away from the nucleus. As a result, they are held in place more weakly. During a chemical reaction, cadmium atoms lose their outer electrons more easily than zinc atoms. Cadmium atoms also take the place of zinc in compounds. In other words, cadmium has a higher reactivity than zinc.

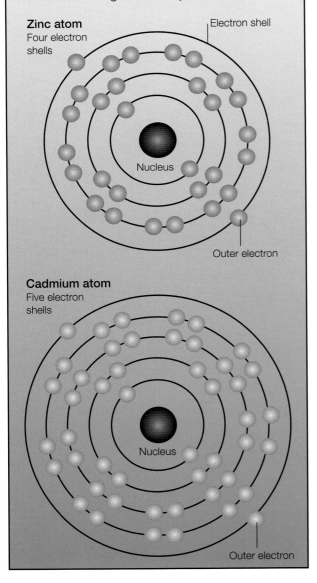

Zinc atom
Four electron shells

Electron shell

Nucleus

Outer electron

Cadmium atom
Five electron shells

Nucleus

Outer electron

an ion with a positive charge, or cation. An atom that gains an electron, becomes a negatively-charged ion, or anion.

Cadmium atoms form ions when they react with the atoms of other elements. During the reaction, the cadmium atom loses its two outer electrons and forms an ion with a charge of +2 (Cd^{2+}). The electrons from the cadmium ion are picked up by atoms of another element.

For example, cadmium reacts with sulfur (S) to form the compound cadmium sulfide (CdS). The sulfur atom gains two electrons from the cadmium atom. It forms a negatively-charged sulfide ion (S^{2-}). Opposite charges attract each other, so the positively-charged cadmium ion is attracted to the negatively-charged sulfur ion. The ions bond together to make cadmium sulfide. Compounds that form in this way are described as ionic.

Cadmium reactions

Cadmium also forms compounds with many other elements. For example, it reacts with oxygen (O_2) to make cadmium oxide (CdO). Cadmium also reacts with chlorine (Cl_2), making cadmium chloride ($CdCl_2$).

Despite being very reactive, cadmium does not react with water (H_2O). Many metals, such as iron, corrode, or rust, when they react with water, but cadmium does not. As a result, cadmium is mixed with iron to prevent the iron from rusting.

Inside a nickel-cadmium battery are stacks of cadmium plates sandwiched between dark-colored nickel compounds.

Cadmium sulfide is also known as cadmium yellow. The compound is a bright yellow color and it was once commonly used in paints. Cadmium sulfide is made by heating cadmium oxide with hydrogen sulfide gas (H_2S).

Nickel-cadmium batteries

Cadmium is used to create electric currents inside nickel-cadmium batteries (Ni-Cd). An electric current occurs when electrons all move in one direction. Ni-Cd batteries produce a current when cadmium reacts with nickel hydroxide, $Ni(OH)_2$. When the reaction is over, the electricity stops. However, Ni-Cd batteries can be recharged and then reused. An electric current from another source will make the reaction between cadmium and nickel hydroxide go in reverse. Then the two substances can react with each other again and produce more electricity.

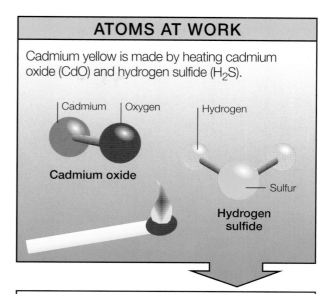

ATOMS AT WORK

Cadmium yellow is made by heating cadmium oxide (CdO) and hydrogen sulfide (H_2S).

Cadmium | Oxygen | Hydrogen

Cadmium oxide

Sulfur

Hydrogen sulfide

During the reaction, the bonds in the cadmium oxide and hydrogen sulfide break, and the atoms rearrange themselves.

Bond breaks

The sulfur and oxygen atoms change places. The oxygen bonds to the hydrogen atoms to form water (H_2O). The sulfur bonds to the cadmium forming cadmium sulfide. That compound forms a yellow powder, which can be collected.

Cadmium sulfide   **Water**

Yellow powder forms

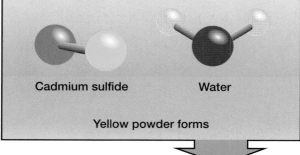

The reaction that takes place can be written like this:

$$H_2S + CdO \rightarrow CdS + H_2O$$

How cadmium is used

Cadmium has many different uses. It is found in a wide variety of products, from the batteries used to power familiar electronic devices to components of nuclear reactors.

Pure cadmium is almost never used on its own. Instead, cadmium is mixed with other metals to make alloys or it is used combined with other elements to form compounds. Alloys containing cadmium are hard wearing—they do not get worn away easily. The alloys also melt at low temperatures compared to most metals. Lastly, cadmium alloys do not rust or corrode quickly.

Most of the cadmium produced is used to make nickel-cadmium batteries. The rest of the cadmium is used for making pigments, for coating metals, in nuclear reactors, and to make plastics harder.

Cadmium pigments

Until the middle of the twentieth century, cadmium was not commonly used. Cadmium compounds were used to tan (strengthen and soften) leather made from animal skins. Cadmium sulfide was also an important pigment (colored chemical). Neither of these uses was widespread, but they were common enough for people to begin to produce cadmium compounds in large amounts.

Cadmium sulfide and cadmium selenide (CdSn) are still sometimes used as pigments. They are both brightly colored—cadmium selenide is a vibrant red. Cadmium sulfide is commonly called

Some yellow paints used by artists contain cadmium sulfide, also known as cadmium yellow. However, cadmium is too poisonous to put in the paints used by children. Children's paints contain other compounds.

cadmium yellow and cadmium selenide is called cadmium red. The compounds were discovered in the 1840s. They are mainly used in high-quality oil paints. Their colors are long lasting and do not fade or change after being used.

Cadmium plating

In the 1950s, people began to use cadmium to electroplate other metals. That made the metals resistant to corrosion allowing the metal objects to last longer. Cadmium-plated metal is especially useful in places, such as in chemical plants, where corrosion is a major problem.

Cadmium plating is an electrochemical process. The metal object to be plated is electrified and dunked into a solution

Metal objects are raised from a tank after being electroplated. Electroplating uses a powerful electric current to coat objects with a layer of metal.

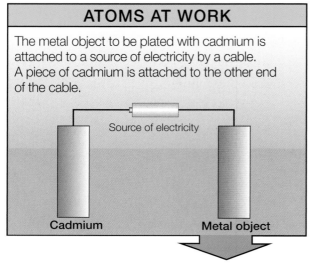

ATOMS AT WORK

The metal object to be plated with cadmium is attached to a source of electricity by a cable. A piece of cadmium is attached to the other end of the cable.

Source of electricity

Cadmium   Metal object

Both pieces of metal are dipped into water containing many dissolved cadmium ions (Cd^{2+}). The current is turned on and flows from the cadmium, through the cable, to the metal object.

Direction of current

Water

Cadmium ion

+2   +2   +2   +2   +2   +2

The electrons in the current are supplied by atoms in the solid cadmium. The atoms become ions and dissolve in the water. These ions are attracted to the other metal object. They turn back into atoms and form a thin layer of cadmium metal on its surface.

Layer of cadmium

The block slowly dissolves.

+2   +2

containing cadmium salts. When cadmium salts are dissolved in water they split into separate ions. The charged cadmium ions are attracted to the electrified metal object. That results in a thin layer of cadmium forming on the metal's surface. This layer of cadmium prevents the metal underneath from corroding—reacting with oxygen, water, or another chemical in the environment.

Nickel-cadmium batteries

About three-quarters of all the cadmium produced is used in nickel-cadmium (Ni-Cd) batteries. Ni-Cd batteries are useful because they can be recharged and reused many times. While they initially cost more than regular batteries, they are less expensive over the long run because they can be recharged many times and do not need to be replaced. Ni-Cd batteries can be used in a wide variety of household products including portable radios, toys, and flashlights.

Ni-Cd batteries are also used in many industrial applications. Ni-Cd batteries are used to power locomotives, electric buses, and even small aircraft. These batteries are much larger than the ones used in homes. There is another difference, too. Household Ni-Cd batteries are used and then recharged after they are drained. However, the Ni-Cd batteries used in motors work differently. They are

A solar panel made from cadmium telluride produces
an electric current when sunlight shines on it.

Substances that can be both conductors and insulators in different conditions are semiconductors.

Cadmium telluride (CdTe) is a semiconductor. It is used to make solar panels. Solar panels are devices that turn the energy in sunlight into electricity. Cadmium telluride solar panels, or cells, are very efficient. They are made by coating plastic with a layer of cadmium telluride. This layer is only a few atoms

constantly being recharged by the energy from the motor. As a result, these batteries produce tiny amounts of cadmium gas. This gas is poisonous. It leaves the battery through vents and escapes into the air.

Ni-Cd batteries are being slowly replaced by nickel metal hydride (NiMH) batteries. NiMH batteries produce larger currents than Ni-Cd ones and they do not contain any toxic cadmium.

Cadmium as a semiconductor

Most metals are good conductors. That means, they carry electric currents and heat well. For example, if one end of a metal bar is heated, the other end soon gets warm, too. Most nonmetals do not behave like this. They are insulators and do not carry electricity or heat easily.

ATOMS AT WORK

When light strikes the surface of a solar cell, an electron is knocked off the semiconductor surface, and a positively-charged hole is formed.

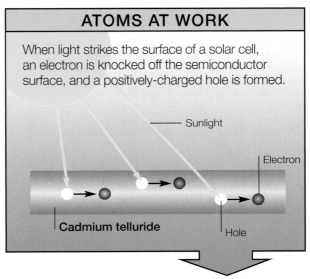

Electrons from the cadmium telluride move across the surface of the solar cell until they enter an electric circuit. Other electrons stream on to the semiconductor from the circuit to fill the electron holes. This process creates the electric current in a solar cell.

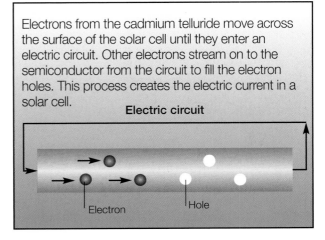

In 1986, one of the reactors at Chernobyl in the Ukraine exploded because it became too hot. The cadmium-containing control rods—like the ones shown here—were not lowered in time.

thick. When sunlight shines on the layer of cadmium telluride, an electric current flows through it. Solar cells like this are used in a wide variety of applications, from powering pocket calculators to generating electricity for whole buildings.

Cadmium in nuclear reactors

Nuclear reactors generate electricity using the heat produced by radioactive uranium as it decays. Neutrons are fired at the uranium fuel in the reactor to make it decay and produce heat. The more neutrons that hit the fuel, the hotter the reactor gets.

If the reactor got too hot it could catch fire or even explode in a process known as a meltdown. To prevent that from happening, the number of neutrons in the reactor must be controlled. That is done using long control rods, which absorb neutrons and stop them from reaching the fuel.

The control rods contain cadmium and some other elements that collect neutrons. When the reactor gets too hot, the control rods are lowered into it to collect some neutrons and slow the decay of uranium. To make the reactor hotter, the rods are lifted out of the reactor.

The nuclear reactor is surrounded by a jacket of cadmium. That prevents neutrons and other dangerous particles or radiation from leaking out.

Cadmium in the environment

Cadmium is a highly poisonous element. If it gets into the environment, it can damage wildlife. If the cadmium gets into drinking water or food, it can affect people's health.

Sources of cadmium

One of the main sources of cadmium pollution are nickel-cadmium (Ni-Cd) batteries that are thrown in the garbage. Although they can be reused many times, eventually the batteries need to be replaced. Most of them are thrown away with the garbage. As a result, the cadmium in the batteries ends up in the ground, where it can get into water and soil.

Each year more than 1,100 tons (1,000 tonnes) of cadmium are used to make Ni-Cd batteries in the United States. A single AA-sized Ni-Cd battery contains about 0.14 ounces (4 g) of cadmium.

The Environmental Protection Agency (EPA) estimates that about a ton of cadmium dust is released into the air each year. Much of this is from Ni-Cd batteries that have been thrown away.

Piles of unwanted waste at an abandoned coal mine in Ohio release cadmium and other pollutants into the nearby water.

In the soil, water, and air

Cadmium levels build up in the air, soil, and water around industrial areas where cadmium is used. Some areas may have very high levels of cadmium. Cadmium dust is very heavy and any dust in the air soon falls to the ground, where it is absorbed by plants. When animals or people eat these plants, the cadmium begins to poison them.

Most cadmium salts are soluble in water so they are easily washed off the land and into streams where they can kill fish and contaminate water supplies.

Other sources of cadmium

Cadmium is known to build up in plants. One of these plants is tobacco, which is used to make cigarettes and cigars. Even though tobacco may contain only small amounts of cadmium, the element is very easily absorbed by human lungs. This can cause cadmium to rapidly build up in the body of a smoker. Cadmium is one of the causes of the diseases that are linked to smoking.

Some phosphate fertilizers may contain large amounts of cadmium. The cadmium is a natural impurity. When these fertilizers are used on crops, the plants will take up the cadmium.

Cadmium exposure levels

Government agencies set limits on how much cadmium can safely be in the environment. For example, the EPA sets the limit for public drinking water supplies. There must not be more than five atoms of cadmium in every billion of atoms in a sample of water (described as 5 parts per billion). The air must have less than 5 micrograms of cadmium per cubic meter. The limit for food is 15 parts per million.

Discarded rechargeable batteries are the main source of cadmium pollution. The batteries should be recycled so the cadmium is reused and not released into the environment.

The level of cadmium in the body can be checked by analyzing blood and urine samples. Long-term exposure is measured by analyzing hair and fingernails.

Common exposure

People may be exposed to cadmium in many different ways. Records indicate that about 90 percent of the exposure to cadmium comes from foods. On average, people consume about 30 micrograms of cadmium every day in their food. However, only about 5 to 10 percent of this is actually absorbed by the body.

A cigarette contains about 1 to 2 micrograms of cadmium. Because cadmium is easily absorbed through the lungs, 60 percent of the cadmium in a cigarette is absorbed. The cadmium absorbed by the lungs is added to the cadmium absorbed from foods. A person who smokes a pack of cigarettes a day gets more than 10 times the amount of cadmium per day as a nonsmoker.

Tobacco plants used to make cigarettes absorb cadmium compounds from the soil. When a person smokes a cigarette, he or she is breathing in dangerous amounts of cadmium along with hundreds of other poisons.

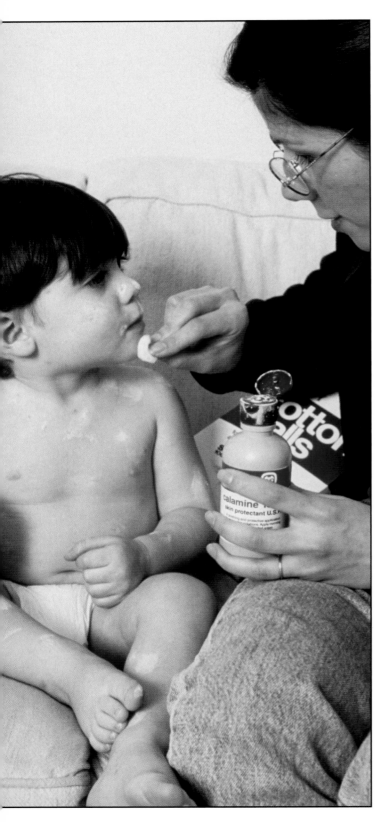

Cadmium and health

Cadmium is one of the few elements that does not serve a purpose in the human body. Cadmium and cadmium compounds are very toxic (poisonous) even at low levels. The health risks is made greater because many cadmium compounds dissolve in water easily so they can get into the blood and other body fluids. Once in the body, cadmium is difficult to remove, and it continues to build up.

Effects on the body

The largest amounts of cadmium builds up in the kidneys. This damages the way kidneys work to remove waste from the blood. That can causes kidney failure, high blood pressure, and heart disease. It may also affect the amount of calcium in the body and cause bones to weaken.

Exposure to high levels of cadmium affects the body's immune system. The immune system protects the body from diseases. High levels of cadmium lead to an increased risk of lung and prostate cancer. Cadmium poisoning may also

A mother applies calamine lotion to a child suffering from chickenpox. The lotion, which contains tiny and harmless amounts of cadmium oxide, soothes the itchy spots caused by the illness.

Soon after World War II (1939–1945), there was a widespread outbreak of cadmium poisoning in Japan. The area where the poisoning occurred was close to where cadmium was being mined. Water from the mine was used to irrigate crops. People developed a disease that they named *itai-itai* disease (the translation is "ouch-ouch" disease). The cadmium was weakening their bones and causing severe pains.

cause pregnant women to give birth to babies early or stop babies from growing fast enough before they are born.

Body chemistry

Copper, zinc, iron, calcium, and vitamin D are all very important to the health of a human body. Most are found in enzymes or work with enzymes to control the body's chemical reactions. Without these enzymes, many of the body's reactions would not take place at all.

Calcium is found in bones but it is also found in many different compounds in the body. Vitamin D takes part in many different chemical reactions in the body. All of these substances react in a similar manner as cadmium. In fact, if the body is

deficient in one or more of these elements, cadmium in the body may become involved in the reaction instead. Because cadmium is toxic, that will be harmful to a person's health.

Symptoms of cadmium poisoning

Short-term exposure to airborne cadmium affects the lungs and breathing. Welders are exposed to cadmium as they work with hot metals.

Long-term exposure results from eating foods or drinking water high in cadmium. The cadmium builds up in the body and begins to damage health. In this type of poisoning, the stomach and intestines are affected first. That causes vomiting and diarrhea. If more cadmium is swallowed a person soon becomes very ill and dies.

The light from lasers is used to remove skin cancers and help other skin problems heal. The purple laser seen here is made using cadmium.

Periodic table

Everything in the universe is made from combinations of substances called elements. Elements are made of tiny atoms, which are the building blocks of matter.

The character of an atom depends on how many even tinier particles called protons there are in its center, or nucleus. An element's atomic number is the same as the number of its protons.

Scientists have found around 116 different elements. About 90 elements occur naturally on Earth. The rest have been made in experiments.

All these elements are set out on a chart called the periodic table. This lists all the elements in order according to their atomic number.

The elements at the left of the table are metals. Those at the right are nonmetals. Between the metals and the nonmetals are the metalloids, which sometimes act like metals and sometimes like nonmetals.

● On the left of the table are the alkali metals. These have just one outer electron.

● Metals get more reactive as you go down a group. The most reactive nonmetals are at the top of the table.

● On the right of the periodic table are the noble gases. These elements have full outer shells.

● The number of electrons orbiting the nucleus increases down each group.

● Elements in the same group have the same number of electrons in their outer shells.

● The transition metals are in the middle of the table, between Groups II and III.

Group I

Group II

Transition metals

1 H Hydrogen 1								
3 Li Lithium 7	4 Be Beryllium 9							
11 Na Sodium 23	12 Mg Magnesium 24							
19 K Potassium 39	20 Ca Calcium 40	21 Sc Scandium 45	22 Ti Titanium 48	23 V Vanadium 51	24 Cr Chromium 52	25 Mn Manganese 55	26 Fe Iron 56	27 Co Cobalt 59
37 Rb Rubidium 85	38 Sr Strontium 88	39 Y Yttrium 89	40 Zr Zirconium 91	41 Nb Niobium 93	42 Mo Molybdenum 96	43 Tc Technetium (98)	44 Ru Ruthenium 101	45 Rh Rhodium 103
55 Cs Cesium 133	56 Ba Barium 137	71 Lu Lutetium 175	72 Hf Hafnium 179	73 Ta Tantalum 181	74 W Tungsten 184	75 Re Rhenium 186	76 Os Osmium 190	77 Ir Iridium 192
87 Fr Francium 223	88 Ra Radium 226	103 Lr Lawrencium (260)	104 Rf Rutherfordium (263)	105 Db Dubnium (268)	106 Sg Seaborgium (266)	107 Bh Bohrium (272)	108 Hs Hassium (277)	109 Mt Meitnerium (276)

Lanthanide elements

Actinide elements

57 La Lanthanum 39	58 Ce Cerium 140	59 Pr Praseodymium 141	60 Nd Neodymium 144	61 Pm Promethium (145)
89 Ac Actinium 227	90 Th Thorium 232	91 Pa Protactinium 231	92 U Uranium 238	93 Np Neptunium (237)

The horizontal rows are called periods. As you go across a period, the atomic number increases by one from each element to the next. The vertical columns are called groups. Elements get heavier as you go down a group. All the elements in a group have the same number of electrons in their outer shells. This means they react in similar ways.

The transition metals fall between Groups II and III. Their electron shells fill up in an unusual way. The lanthanide elements and the actinide elements are set apart from the main table to make it easier to read. All the lanthanide elements and the actinide elements are quite rare.

Cadmium in the table

Cadmium is a transition metal. Most transition metals have an unfilled electron shell below their outer shell. However, cadmium is unusual because all of its shells are full except for its outer one. Cadmium shares this characteristic with zinc and mercury, the elements that are located above and below cadmium in the table.

Metals
Metalloids (semimetals)
Nonmetals

48
Cd
Cadmium
112

Atomic (proton) number
Symbol
Name
Atomic mass

			Group III	Group IV	Group V	Group VI	Group VII	Group VIII
								2 He Helium 4
			5 B Boron 11	6 C Carbon 12	7 N Nitrogen 14	8 O Oxygen 16	9 F Fluorine 19	10 Ne Neon 20
			13 Al Aluminum 27	14 Si Silicon 28	15 P Phosphorus 31	16 S Sulfur 32	17 Cl Chlorine 35	18 Ar Argon 40
28 Ni Nickel 59	29 Cu Copper 64	30 Zn Zinc 65	31 Ga Gallium 70	32 Ge Germanium 73	33 As Arsenic 75	34 Se Selenium 79	35 Br Bromine 80	36 Kr Krypton 84
46 Pd Palladium 106	47 Ag Silver 108	48 Cd Cadmium 112	49 In Indium 115	50 Sn Tin 119	51 Sb Antimony 122	52 Te Tellurium 128	53 I Iodine 127	54 Xe Xenon 131
78 Pt Platinum 195	79 Au Gold 197	80 Hg Mercury 201	81 Tl Thallium 204	82 Pb Lead 207	83 Bi Bismuth 209	84 Po Polonium (209)	85 At Astatine (210)	86 Rn Radon (222)
110 Ds Darmstadtium (281)	111 Rg Roentgenium (280)	112 Uub Ununbium (285)	113 Uut Ununtrium (284)	114 Uuq Ununquadium (289)	115 Uup Ununpentium (288)	116 Uuh Ununhexium (292)		

62 Sm Samarium 150	63 Eu Europium 152	64 Gd Gadolinium 157	65 Tb Terbium 159	66 Dy Dysprosium 163	67 Ho Holmium 165	68 Er Erbium 167	69 Tm Thulium 169	70 Yb Ytterbium 173
94 Pu Plutonium (244)	95 Am Americium (243)	96 Cm Curium (247)	97 Bk Berkelium (247)	98 Cf Californium (251)	99 Es Einsteinium (252)	100 Fm Fermium (257)	101 Md Mendelevium (258)	102 No Nobelium (259)

Chemical reactions

Chemical reactions are going on around us all the time. Some reactions involve just two substances, while others involve many more. But whenever a reaction takes place, at least one substance is changed. In a chemical reaction, the numbers and types of atoms stay the same. But they join up in different combinations to form new molecules.

Writing an equation

Chemical reactions can be described by writing down the atoms and molecules before and after the reaction. Since the

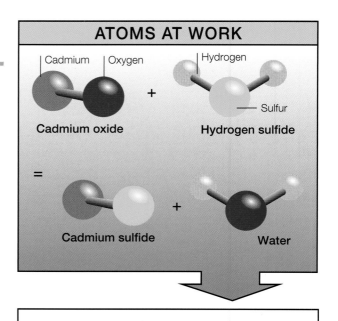

ATOMS AT WORK

Cadmium | Oxygen   Hydrogen

Cadmium oxide   Sulfur

Hydrogen sulfide

=

Cadmium sulfide   +   **Water**

The reaction that takes place when cadmium oxide reacts with hydrogen sulfide is written like this:

$$H_2S + CdO \rightarrow CdS + H_2O$$

This tells us that a molecule of hydrogen sulfide reacts with a molecule of cadmium oxide to give one molecule of cadmium sulfide and one molecule of water.

This light-sensitive resistor contains cadmium telluride. When light shines on this component, it allows more electricity to flow through it.

atoms stay the same, the number of atoms before the reaction will be the same as the number of atoms after. Chemists write the reaction as an equation. This shows what happens in the chemical reaction.

Making it balance

When the numbers of each atom on both sides of the equation are equal, the equation is balanced. If the numbers are not equal, something is wrong. So the chemist adjusts the number of atoms involved until the equation balances.

Glossary

acid: An acid is a chemical that releases hydrogen ions easily during reactions.

atom: The smallest part of an element that has all the properties of that element.

atomic mass number: The number of protons and neutrons in an atom.

atomic number: The number of protons in an atom's nucleus. Each element has a unique atomic number.

bond: The attraction between two atoms, or ions, that holds them together.

compound: A substance made of two or more elements chemically joined together.

corrosion: The eating away of a material by reaction with other chemicals, often oxygen and moisture in the air.

electrolysis: The use of electricity to change a substance chemically.

electron: A tiny particle with a negative charge. Electrons are found inside atoms, where they move around the nucleus in layers called electron shells.

element: A substance that is made from only one type of atom.

ion: An atom or a group of atoms that has lost or gained electrons to become electrically charged.

mineral: A compound or element as it is found in its natural form in Earth.

metal: An element on the left-hand side of the periodic table.

molecule: A unit that contains atoms held together by chemical bonds.

nonmetal: An element on the right-hand side of the periodic table.

nucleus: The dense structure at the center of an atom containing protons and neutrons.

neutron: A tiny particle with no electrical charge. Neutrons are found in the nucleus of almost every atom.

ore: A mineral or rock that contains enough of a particular substance to make it useful for mining.

periodic table: A chart of all the chemical elements laid out in order of their atomic number.

proton: A tiny particle with a positive charge. Protons are found in the nucleus.

radiation: Particles and rays produced when a radioactive element decays.

radioactivity: A property of certain unstable atoms that causes them to release radiation.

reaction: A process in which two or more elements or compounds combine to produce new substances.

semiconductor: A substance that is sometimes a good conductor of electricity and sometimes a poor conductor of electricity.

transition metal: An element positioned in the middle of the periodic table. As well as having spaces in their outer electron shell, most transition metals also have spaces in the next outermost shell.

Index